Rickshaw Reggie

CHICAGO NEIGHBORHOODS

WRITTEN BY KATHLEEN DRAGAN
ILLUSTRATED BY ED KOEHLER

Copyright © 2017, Reedy Press, LLC
All rights reserved.
Reedy Press
PO Box 5131
St. Louis, MO 63139
www.reedypress.com

No part of this publication may be reproduced or transmitted in any form or by any means,
electronic or mechanical, including photocopy, recording, or any information storage and retrieval system,
without permission in writing from the publisher. Permissions may be sought directly from Reedy Press
at the above mailing address or via our website at www.reedypress.com.

Library of Congress Control Number: 2017934684
ISBN: 9781681060767

Printed in the United States of America
18 19 20 21   5 4 3 2

"Now hopefully that luck can help us find a taxi . . ."

"Catching a foul ball at my first Cubs game—
I can't believe my luck!"

"If it's a ride you're after, I've got room for a few.
And if you're looking for excitement, then you're in luck too."

"Who are you?" said Charlie.

"And what is that thing you're operating?" asked Grandma.

"This old beauty might be short on chrome,
    but we'll give you the REAL tour before we fly you home.
Baseball's great, don't mean to put it down.
    But there's a whole lot more to explore in this town."

past. In Lincoln Park you'll have a blast.

Peggy Notebaert Nature Center: Enter the butterfly room as you are, but make sure they haven't tried to hitch a ride out on your clothes!

North Pond Nature Sanctuary

Elks Memorial

Kingston Mines: What's your blues name? Jelly Roll Morton? Find out here! Mine's just Rickshaw Reggie.

Abraham Lincoln Elementary: Once housed refugees from the Great Chicago Fire in 1871.

Green City Market: If you're willing to try a vegetable at this year-round farmers market, you can join Club Sprouts and earn a prize!

Lincoln Park Conservatory: Find the hidden dinosaurs in the fern room, or warm up during the holidays and watch the miniature trains.

Alfred Caldwell Lily Pond

The Wieners Circle: A char dog with the works: tomatoes, pickles, onions, celery salt, mustard, relish, and sport peppers. No ketchup.

Lincoln Park Zoo: Say hi to my animal friends, like Alexander Camelton. It won't cost you a dime. There's a burr oak tree by the monkey house that's older than the city itself.

Original Ferris Wheel: Stood at Clark and Wrightwood from 1896 to 1903. (Now it's a McDonald's.)

ChicagoHistoryMuseum

Policeman Bellinger's Cottage: How he saved his cottage from the Great Chicago Fire is one of history's mysteries.

Chicago History Museum: History comes to life here. Climb onto the first "L" car: it once ran from the Loop to Hyde Park. But I can get you there faster now.

Midwest Buddhist Temple: Japanese Americans built this temple in 1944. I go to the Legacy Garden when I need a little peace and quiet.

W NORTH AV
1600 N

North Avenue: Once the northern boundary of Chicago, the city had to buy more land for smallpox quarantine.

Phillip Rogers Toll Gate: Back when folks rode in stagecoaches, Mr. Phillip Rogers had the bright idea to set up a toll gate here. No I-pass accepted.

80 Different Languages: They say that's how many are spoken by Rogers Park natives. It just might be the most diverse neighborhood in the whole U.S.A.

Marion Mahoney Griffin: One of the first licensed female architects in the world. They say she even helped Mr. Frank Lloyd Wright with a good bit of his portfolio.

Indian Boundary Park: Once this housed a pretty fine zoo. The swan houses are still there and you can play in them too!

Harold Ramis: No wonder Rogers Park isn't haunted. One of the original Ghostbusters grew up here!

AUG 14
Pakistani Independence Day

Pakistani Independence Day Parade: Celebrated each year on August 14th.

Thillens

Thillens Stadium: When I played baseball here as a tot, a giant spinning baseball statue marked the spot.

ROGERS PARK WEST RIDGE

India Town: Try new foods at an Indian buffet. Just don't forget to save room for Kheer and Mango Kulfi.

Robert A. Black Golf Course

DEVON AVENUE

Tel-Aviv Kosher Bakery: They might give you a sample cookie if you stop in here.

Devon Avenue: Stores range from Indian and Pakistani to Russian and Kosher Jewish. It's like going around the world without leaving one street.

...ee lots of art, and open your mind.

Mile of Murals: Start at the Howard L stop and walk south. You'll see a mile of murals tucked under the tracks.

Howard CTA Stop: Last stop in the city on a northbound train.

Emil Bach House: A Frank Lloyd Wright mansion, prairie style.

North end of Western: At 23.5 miles, Western's the longest street in the city. Here's the northern end. Stay tuned for the southern!

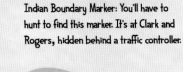

Indian Boundary Marker: You'll have to hunt to find this marker. It's at Clark and Rogers, hidden behind a traffic controller.

Artists of the Wall: 600 feet of community murals. They start all over every year on Father's Day.

Loyola Beach

Glenwood Ave. Arts District: Cobblestone streets and Sunday markets, you'll find something interesting that catches your eye.

Dune Preservation: Five different endangered plants are getting a chance to thrive in this spot. It's starting to look the way nature intended it, again.

JB Alberto's Pizza: The pizza here's famous, but I like the liter of RC Cola that comes with my order.

Cracker Jack's: Introduced in 1893 at the World's Fair, the model for the sailor boy was the grandson of inventor Frederick William Rueckheim, who lived around here.

Loyola University

"We kind of took off without much of a warning,
but I promise I'll get you both home by morning."

"I said airbags, not airborne. Return us to solid ground this instant!"

"But Grandma, I never would have noticed all those places."

"Buckle up and hold on tight.

We've got a lot more neighborhoods to visit tonight!"

Turn Left

Bungalows, churches, and hug

Dunham Park

2,000 %
Around the turn of the 20th century, Chicago's population increased more than 2000%, so they annexed more land and encouraged folks to move out of congested downtown.

Frogtown: This area was once known as Frogtown because every spring it was one big pond.

Hagen's Fish Market: A Scandanavian breakfast? That's smoked fish on toast. Stock up here.

What is a portage?: The land between two bodies of water is a portage. Native Americans loved this one between the Des Plaines and Chicago rivers because it was so swampy they could stay in their canoes to paddle across.

Portage Park pool: An outdoor Olympic-sized pool with high dives was built for the 1959 Pan American games. They used it again for the 1972 Olympic trials, and World Records were broken here!

PATIO

Patio Theater: Look up at the ceiling: it's just like the night sky!

Green Limousines: CTA replaced trolleys with buses in 1973. We called them "green limousines."

BELMONT BUSINESS DISTRICT

Casimir Pulaski: Twice a war hero, in Poland and our Revolutionary War, Chicago school kids used to get the day off of school for his March 6th birthday.

Belmont Central Business District: The highest concentration of Polish stores for the highest concentration of Polish people in Chicago.

Chopin Park: Named for the Polish composer and child prodigy who was playing piano concerts by the time he was seven.

paces to play, but what is a "portage" anyway?

Our Lady of Victory

Fantasy Costumes: With over 1,000,000 pieces to choose from, you're bound to find the right costume— I wonder if they have a Rickshaw Reggie outfit?

BBQ FEST

BBQ Fest

6 Corners Shopping District: Count the corners just to check their math. This was the largest shopping district outside of downtown.

Dickinson's Tavern: Once stood at Dickinson and Belle Plaine and hosted the likes of Abraham Lincoln and Stephen Douglas when they would travel through Illinois.

Portage Theater: One of the oldest movie theaters in Chicago.

SIX CORNERS

SEARS

SEARS: This was one of the first stores for the catalog company, and it opened its doors to 100,000 eager shoppers on opening day.

The Bungalow Belt: One in three houses in Chicago is built in this cozy style. Most were built between 1910 and 1940.

Pączki: Pick up a dozen of these Polish fried doughnuts filled with Powid! or rose hip jam on Fat Tuesday. Pronounce it PAWNCH-key and maybe they'll throw in an extra one.

PORTAGE PARK

Head on down to the Lower West Side

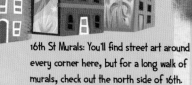

A
18 ST.

Ashland pink/green lines

16th St Murals: You'll find street art around every corner here, but for a long walk of murals, check out the north side of 16th.

18th St: "La Diecioho" is the place to browse galleries, pick up your sugar skulls for Day of the Dead, and try some of the most authentic Mexican food in the country.

Día de los Muertos: You'll see skeletons, altars, and sugar skulls around every bend during this celebration of loved ones who have passed.

National Museum of Mexican Art: Largest of its kind in the nation.

Benito Juarez Community Academy: The statues honor Mexican heroes, the mural's called "Hope," and the whole high school was built to look like an Aztec temple.

Heart of Chicago's Italian hub: Two blocks of northern Italian restaurants from the city's original Little Italy.

Elote: Sweet Midwest corn meets the Mexican style of eating it with chile, lime, salt, butter, mayo, and cheese.

Fiesta del Sol: Three days of summer fun, it's the largest Latino festival in the Midwest.

Paletas: Mexican popsicles with chunks of fresh fruit. My favorite is the mango with chile.

Fiesta del Sol

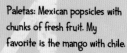

Plzeň (Pilsen)

Plzeň: The neighborhood takes its name after a city in the Czech Republic, because the first residents here traced their roots to Bohemia.

The floating staircases: See how the stairs go right up to the second floor? When the streets were raised in Chicago, they just built a new front door and a new set of stairs instead of raising the whole house.

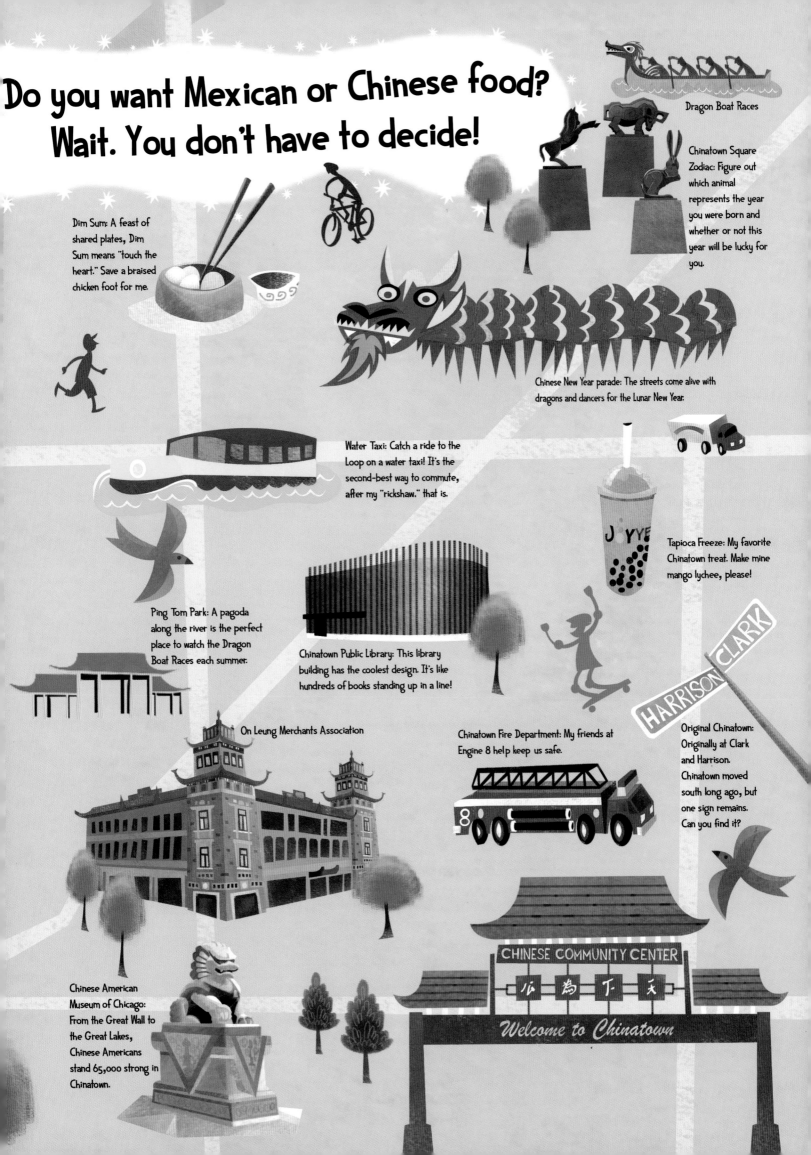

Do you want Mexican or Chinese food? Wait. You don't have to decide!

Dragon Boat Races

Chinatown Square Zodiac: Figure out which animal represents the year you were born and whether or not this year will be lucky for you.

Dim Sum: A feast of shared plates, Dim Sum means "touch the heart." Save a braised chicken foot for me.

Chinese New Year parade: The streets come alive with dragons and dancers for the Lunar New Year.

Water Taxi: Catch a ride to the Loop on a water taxi! It's the second-best way to commute, after my "rickshaw." that is.

Tapioca Freeze: My favorite Chinatown treat. Make mine mango lychee, please!

Ping Tom Park: A pagoda along the river is the perfect place to watch the Dragon Boat Races each summer.

Chinatown Public Library: This library building has the coolest design. It's like hundreds of books standing up in a line!

HARRISON CLARK

On Leung Merchants Association

Chinatown Fire Department: My friends at Engine 8 help keep us safe.

Original Chinatown: Originally at Clark and Harrison. Chinatown moved south long ago, but one sign remains. Can you find it?

Chinese American Museum of Chicago: From the Great Wall to the Great Lakes, Chinese Americans stand 65,000 strong in Chinatown.

CHINESE COMMUNITY CENTER

小 為 丁 大

Welcome to Chinatown

"Why did so many different people come to live in Chicago?"
Charlie asked.

"What you've got here is a city of tales.
    Some came with family, some came to work the rails.
Hardworking folks moved here from all over.
    That earned us the name "The City of BIG Shoulders."

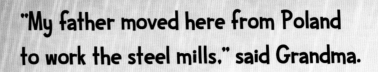

"My father moved here from Poland to work the steel mills," said Grandma.

"I never knew that!" said Charlie.

JANSON'S
DRIVE-IN
HAMBURGERS
RED HOTS

HOT HOMEMADE SOUP

Janson's Drive-In: No longer a drive-in, I'd still recommend a dine-in.

The Original Rainbow Cone: All the ice cream flavors? It's a poor orphan's dream come true. More than 90 years of the wildest combo of flavors you have to try to believe: chocolate, strawberry, Palmer House, pistachio, orange sherbet.

South Side Irish: After the Great Chicago Fire, many Irish families moved south; it's still one of the largest ethnic groups represented in the city.

South Side Irish St. Patrick's Day Parade: There might not be a green river in Beverly, but the South Side Irish pride flows freely on this day each year.

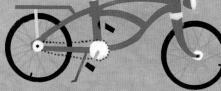

Schwinn Bicycles: Putting us all on two wheels since 1895, thanks to Beverly resident Mr. Ignaz Schwinn.

Italian Beef: Know how to order this sandwich: hot dipped, sweet dry, or cheef. Just don't forget the extra napkins—you'll need them.

Horse Thief Hollow: Legend has it this area used to be a hideout for bandits and the horses they stole.

HIGHEST POINT IN CHICAGO

Set on top of a ridge, this is the highest natural point. But at just 672 ft. above sea level, it's not exactly Mt. Everest.

Southern End of Western: 23.5 miles total, we're about ten blocks from the southern end of Western, the longest street in the city.

Beverly Arts Center

Welcome to BEVERLY HILLS

Rock Island Metra: It might feel like you're a million miles from the city, but Rock Island Metra will get you downtown in a jiffy.

Big Families: Families with five kids or more? That's nothing rare around here.

Village in the City: Tree-lined streets with mansions give this neighborhood a real small-town feel.

St. Margaret of Scotland: Beverly has four Catholic churches, and a school to go with each.

Civil Servants: There's a long history of police officers, firefighters, and teachers making their homes in Beverly.

Beverly Unitarian Church: Built in 1886, this was designed to look just like an Irish castle between Dublin and Belfast.

George Pullman built train car
In this old factory tow

National A. Philip Randolph Pullman Porter Museum: A unique museum dedicated to African Americans' contributions to the labor movement.

Hotel Florence: Named for Mr. Pullman's oldest daughter.

Brotherhood of Pullman Porters: First chartered African American labor organization, they fought for better wages and fair treatment.

National Park: In 2015, Pullman became Chicago's first National Park.

Metra Electric Line: It might not be a Pullman Palace Car, but the Metra Electric line will make the twelve-mile trip downtown fly by.

Pullman Visitor Center: Stop in here to learn about the "Workers' Paradise" the Pullman Company built here in the 1880s.

Stables

Gotham Greens: Urban agricultural company growing fresh greens right here. They even named their lettuce after Pullman.

Arcade Row: The arcade was a huge indoor market, one of the country's first malls!

here people could sleep.
he history runs deep.

Highway 94: In Chicago the roads have names and numbers. This one is the Bishop Ford.

94

Pullman Clock Tower and Factory: If you lived in Pullman, this is where you clocked into work. It was the model for Santa's village in the *Polar Express* movie too!

PULLMAN

Market Square

Executive Row

Foreman's Row

Arcade Park

SEPTEMBER

Labor Day: That first Monday in September when you say goodbye to summer with a cookout at the beach? That's a holiday thanks to the workers of Pullman!

Calumet: So what is a calumet? It's the French word used to describe a Native American ceremonial pipe.

Greenstone Church: The stone it's made of is called "serpentine limestone." I bet you can see why.

Lake Calumet: The largest body of water in the city of Chicago.

"I'm seeing parts of Chicago I didn't know existed...
and I've lived here my whole life," said Grandma.

"You mean this is new to you, too?" said Charlie.

"Travel a few streets and the landscape looks foreign.
I see it all so I take folks exploring.
Names and faces change through the years.
Each block tells a story if you're willing to lend an ear."

Two presidents have worked here nuclear energy was discovered

Harold Washington: He lived here while serving as the city's first African American mayor. The downtown library named after him was once the largest public library in the world.

KAM Isaiah Israel: The oldest Jewish congregation west of Ohio: Chicago has the third-largest Jewish population in the U.S.

Home of President Barack Obama: You can sneak a peek at the former Commander-in-Chief's Kenwood home, but don't get too close or security will turn you around.

Oriental Institute: What's cooler than seeing mummies? Getting to mummify one! Each year around Halloween, you can do just that at the Oriental Institute.

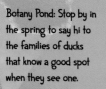

Botany Pond: Stop by in the spring to say hi to the families of ducks that know a good spot when they see one.

Regenstein Library

Valois: It's a cafeteria-style diner. What you see is what you get. And what you get is a lot of good food! Just ask President Obama. It's one of his favorites.

University of Chicago: All the Gothic architecture makes this campus feel like an old castle, where knowledge is King.

DuSable Museum of African American History: Lots to learn here. My favorite part is Harold Washington's office.

57th Street Books

Frederick C. Robie House: Do you think you can design buildings like Frank Lloyd Wright? Once a month you can come here and give it your best shot, with Legos of course.

Fountain of Time Statue

Skating Rink

HYDE PARK
KENWOOD

MIDWAY PLAISANCE PARK

ART
Hyde Park Art Center

Muhammad Ali: Kenwood has had some famous residents, like boxing legend, Muhammad Ali.

Medici on 57th

Bixler Park

COLUMBIAN 1893 EXPOSITION

1893 Chicago World's Fair: They built a whole white city to showcase some amazing new things: the first Ferris Wheel, electricity, and those long flat pennies used for souvenirs.

"Monsters of the Midway": When U of C had a football team, this was its nickname. Now most people mean Da Bears when they say it.

Promontory Point Park: Locals know you call this "the Point." They also know it's one of the best spots to watch the Navy Pier fireworks every weekend.

Original site of first Ferris Wheel

Obama Presidential Center: On the grounds of what was once the Horticultural Building from the World's Fair, a library and foundation will be built in honor of our 44th president.

Museum of Science and Industry: With 2000 exhibits, this is the largest science museum in this whole hemisphere! My favorite is the baby chicks that hatch right in front of you.

PRESIDENT OBAMA LIBRARY

Masaryk Memorial: Honors the first president of Czechoslovakia, Tomas Masaryk, who once taught at the University of Chicago.

Osaka Garden

Wooded Island

Bronzeville's full of greystone
I can almost hear Satchm

Illinois Institute of Technology

Monument to the Great Northern Migration: This friendly statue pays tribute to the thousands of African Americans who moved to Chicago for greater opportunities. What's in his suitcase? I think it's full of dreams.

Miss Bronze America pageant: The beauty contest that gave the neighborhood its name.

Chicago Bee Building: Once the home of Anthony Overton's successful ventures in publishing and cosmetics, now it's a public library.

Pilgrim Baptist Church: Credited as the birthplace of gospel music.

Bronzeville Walk of Fame: The sidewalks of King Drive are dotted with 91 bronze plaques honoring notable African Americans. Look for Gwendolyn Brooks and Louis Armstrong, among many others.

Pearl's Place: One of the best for Southern-style comfort food. Catfish or fried chicken: how can I choose?

White Sox: Their stadium is in Bridgeport, but that's right next door. And those fireworks after home runs might just shake your floor!

Ida B. Wells-Barnett House: Born a slave in Mississippi, she spent her whole life advocating for equal rights.

Abundance Bakery: It'll be hard not to buy everything you see in here, but the caramel upside down cake knocks me right off my feet.

Many of the greats of Jazz, Blues, and Gospel music performed in Bronzeville.

Robert S. Abbott: Home of the founder of the Chicago Defender—once the largest African American newspaper in the country.

...urches, and statues.
...till singing the blues.

Bronzeville sign

Interesting Benches: Finding one of these benches to sit on makes waiting for the bus a lot more fun. Look for them up and down King Dr.

Stephen A. Douglas Tomb: This monument to Lincoln's great rival is the oldest memorial in Illinois.

Victory Monument: Honors an African American regiment that fought in World War I. The soldier on top? He's called a "doughboy." Look down and find a bronze map of the neighborhood!

31ST ST. BEACH

Chicago Lakefront Trail: 18.5 miles of path for walking, running, or biking ... and a great place to find my friend Kathleen.

BUD BILLIKEN

Bud Billiken Parade: The second Saturday in August, the street shuts down for this back-to-school bash.

Harold Washington Cultural Center

Liberty Baptist Church: In the 1960s Dr. Martin Luther King, Jr. spoke here calling for housing equality in the city, and you couldn't find an empty seat—not even in the aisles.

Drexel Fountain: The oldest public statue in the city.

Chicago Flag: The top stripe is the lake, the bottom one's the river, and each star's an important event: Fort Dearborn, the Great Chicago Fire, and two World's Fairs. Will we ever add a fifth star? Time will tell!

Provident Hospital: First African American owned and operated hospital in America, under the guidance of Dr. Daniel Hale Williams.

"Heads up now, it's time to land.
    I told you this journey would be far from bland.
Keep asking questions about the places you see.
    The adventure never ends in your home—your city."

Prepare
for
Landing

"Point the way to bed, Grandma. I'm so tired."

"Not me," said Grandma. "I'm totally wired!
He's even got me rhyming now!"

"We've seen a lot today, but this was just a peek.
To explore Chicago, don't hide—go seek!"

"Help me find the parts I dropped
so I can prepare for my next adventure!"

For Grant, Bailey, and Declan: my team of urban explorers.